WELCOME

Over the past 15 years, Taylor Swift has evolved from a teen country-pop sensation to a genre-shifting, chart-topping global superstar. In this special edition, we relive Taylor's incredible story so far and celebrate the many milestones of her trailblazing career.

Follow Taylor's journey, from her self-titled debut, through to the retro pop of *1989*, the poetic indie of *folklore* and *evermore*, and the recent nostalgia-infused re-recordings of her classic albums. Whatever Taylor does next, we'll be ready for it!

What's more, we'll get to know the woman behind the music. Learn more about Taylor's childhood, friendships and relationships, and see how they have inspired her songwriting. We'll also discover why Taylor is determined to be a force for good in the world, and explore the many ways in which she supports the causes she believes in.

CONTENTS

Making It

Taylor first fell in love with music during her childhood and teenage years, with enthusiastic encouragement and support from her family

Taylor's meteoric rise to fame began as a child when she took a keen interest in musical theatre. Named after singer-songwriter James Taylor, she was destined for a career in music and, unsurprisingly, her early life and first steps into the music industry have always intrigued fans. So, who is Taylor? And how did she make it?

Taylor's childhood & family life

Taylor Alison Swift was born on 13 December 1989 in Reading Hospital in West Reading, Pennsylvania, to parents Scott Kingsley Swift and Andrea Gardner Swift. Growing up, Taylor spent her earlier years on a Christmas tree farm bought by her father, and attended both the Alvernia Montessori School and the Wyndcroft School, both located in Pennsylvania

She took an avid interest in performing and musical theatre from the age of nine, and performed in four productions at Berks Youth Theatre Academy. Her talent led her to take up acting and vocal lessons in New York City, and when she was in the fourth grade, Taylor's talents for lyricism were fostered when she won a national poetry competition for her poem, 'A Monster in My Closet!' ▶▶

Taylor performing in Kansas City, May 2007.

Images: Getty

7

After moving to Wyomissing in Pennsylvania, Taylor was enrolled in Wyomissing Area Junior/Senior High School. She spent an entire summer writing a 350-page novel, which remains unpublished to this day, but enabled her to explore her writing abilities. Taylor had a difficult time at school and was subjected to bullying by her fellow classmates. In March 2009, she graced the cover of *Teen Vogue*, and revealed her experiences, explaining: "Junior high was actually sort of hard because I got dumped by this group of popular girls." She added: "They didn't think I was cool or pretty enough, so they stopped talking to me." During the interview, she also spoke about how the girls had shown up to one of her shows wearing her t-shirts and asking for her autograph: "It was bittersweet, because it made me realize that they didn't remember being mean to me and that I needed to forget about it, too."

However, in true Taylor-style, she turned a negative experience into a positive one. During the interview, she reflected on the struggles she faced at school, and said, "Really, if I hadn't come home from school miserable every day, maybe I wouldn't have been so motivated to write songs. I should probably thank them!"

Taylor's musical influences & her career beginnings

During her childhood, Taylor was heavily influenced by a variety of iconic artists, but it was a member of her own family who gave her the inspiration to sing. Taylor has previously cited her maternal grandmother, the opera

Scott, Taylor and Andrea Swift pictured at the 48th Annual Academy of Country Music Awards in 2013.

singer and television personality Marjorie Finlay, as her inspiration for pursuing her career in music. She has even paid tribute to her grandmother on her song 'marjorie', taken from her ninth studio album, *evermore*. The track even featured sampled backing vocals credited to Marjorie.

Taylor became enamoured with Shania Twain, which led to her interest in country music. Previously, Taylor has said Twain's songs made her "want to just run around the block four times and daydream about everything." Taylor also credits Tina Turner and LeAnn Rimes as early influences. She continued performing throughout her childhood, with shows at local karaoke competitions, festivals and events. But after seeing a documentary on Faith Hill, Taylor wanted to relocate to Nashville in Tennessee – the spiritual home of country music.

At 11 years old, Taylor and her mother visited record labels in Nashville with demo tapes featuring covers of songs by The Chicks and Dolly Parton. While Taylor received rejections, it gave her the drive to aspire to create her own brand of country music, and she later explained: "Everyone in that town wanted ▶▶

Taylor and her mother, Andrea, at the 42nd Annual Academy of Country Music Awards in May 2007.

Taylor singing the national anthem at a Thanksgiving day football game between the Miami Dolphins and Detroit Lions in November 2006.

Images: Getty

9

Performing at the CMA Music Festival in Nashville, Tennessee, June 2007.

to do what I wanted to do. So, I kept thinking to myself, I need to figure out a way to be different."

Taylor continued to home in on her talent for live performances, and at 12 years old, she performed at a Philadelphia 76ers basketball game in the spring of 2002, with her rendition of 'The Star-Spangled Banner', the national anthem of the United States. It was during this time that Taylor learnt how to play the guitar, and received lessons from a local musician called Ronnie Cremer, who taught her how to play her first three chords (C, D and G). Cremer also helped Taylor learn how to write songs, and she soon wrote her first track, 'Lucky You', inspired by her grandmother, Marjorie.

After performing the national anthem at the 2003 US Open at the age of 13, she began working with Dan Dymtrow, a talent manager based in New York, and joined Abercrombie & Fitch's 'Rising Stars' campaign as a model. Her partnership with Dymtrow also led to the inclusion of one of her songs on a Maybelline compilation CD, and the opportunity to meet with major record labels, as well as an artist development deal with RCA Records.

Taylor continued to visit Nashville with her mother in an attempt to break into the music industry there, and her family enthusiastically encouraged her career. Her father relocated to the Nashville office of Merrill (the American investment management firm where he worked as a stockbroker) when she was 14 years old. Taylor enrolled at Hendersonville High School, but when her touring schedule became busier, she transferred to Aaron Academy, which helped her accommodate her music career and her schooling, before she graduated a year early. These early teenage years, which saw Taylor find her footing as a solo artist, provided the backdrop for her first record deal, and the launch of her music career.

Record deal & debut album
At the age of 14, Taylor signed with Sony/ATV Tree publishing house as a songwriter and became ▶▶

> "Taylor continued to visit Nashville in an attempt to break into the music industry, and her family enthusiastically encouraged her career.

the youngest signee in the company's history. Taylor began travelling between Hendersonville and Nashville, and worked with Music Row songwriters including Brett James, Troy Verges and the Warren Brothers, as well as Elisabeth Wagner (known professionally as Liz Rose), who would go on to co-write 17 of Taylor's released songs.

While she signed a development deal with the Sony Music Entertainment-owned label RCA Records when she was 14, she decided to part ways with the label over creative differences, which were stopping her from performing her own original songs. In a 2009 interview with *The Daily Telegraph*, Taylor explained the decision, saying, "I genuinely felt that I was running out of time. I wanted to capture these years of my life on an album while they still represented what I was going through."

It wasn't long before she was able to begin a new partnership: after performing at the Bluebird Café in Nashville in 2005, Taylor was scouted by Scott Borchetta. Borchetta, a DreamWorks Records executive at the time, was preparing to start his own independent record label, Big Machine Records. Taylor joined the label as one of its first signees, and her father bought a 3% stake in the company for around $120,000. Taylor began working on her self-titled debut album and wrote three of the album's songs on her own, co-writing the remaining eight tracks with Liz Rose, Brian Maher, Robert Ellis Orrall and Angelo Petraglia.

The album's lead single, 'Tim McGraw', was released in June 2006. Its narrative centred on a summer romance that comes to an abrupt end, using country star Tim McGraw's music as a reference to the relationships' timeline. The song was released to critical acclaim, with *AllMusic*'s Jeff Tamarkin remarking that the song showed Taylor as "a talent to be reckoned with," and *Country Standard Time*'s Rick Bell called it an "impressive debut."

After her debut album was released in October 2006, Taylor promoted the record with a radio tour and opened for Rascal Flatts during some of their shows on their 2006 tour. Taylor's appearance came after Rascal Flatts fired their original opening act, Eric Church, as he was playing for longer than planned during his support slots. Church jokingly told Taylor that she should gift him her first gold record to say thanks for the opportunity created by his dismissal. He may have only said it in jest,

Taylor poses during an early-career appearance on a weekday morning news show in October 2006.

Images: Getty, Shutterstock

Singing the national anthem
at the Los Angeles Dodgers
and Colorado Rockies
baseball game in April 2007.

A shocked Taylor accepts the Breakthrough Video of the Year award for 'Tim McGraw' at the CMT Music Awards, April 2007.

Critics praised Taylor's songwriting ability and lauded her debut album's maturity.

intelligence and idealism," and *The Palm Beach Post*'s Janis Fontaine reflected on the album's "musical maturity". However, some critics gave the record mixed reviews, with *PopMatters*' Roger Holland writing "It's to be hoped that when she finds both her place and her full-grown voice, she's able to find an accommodation between the country tradition and her very obvious pop sensibilities."

Taylor's self-titled debut album entered at a respectable number 19 on the *Billboard* 200. However, the album continued to sell and by November 2007, more than a million copies of *Taylor Swift* had been sold. The album peaked at number five on the *Billboard* 200 in late-January 2008, and by October 2009, the record had spent more time on the chart than any other album released in the 2000s. *Taylor Swift* peaked at number one on the *Billboard* Top Country Albums chart, spending 24 weeks in the top spot. But for Taylor, these were just the first achievements in what would become a very long list of incredible career triumphs.

Taylor's interest in music and incredible work ethic meant that she had finished recording her debut by the end of her first year of high school. With the support and encouragement from her parents from a young age – as well as the local opportunities given to her and the potential that industry experts such as Dymtrow and Borchetta saw in her – Taylor was able to lay the foundations for a solo career that would take the world by storm.

Taylor poses with her trophy in the press room at the 2007 CMT Music Awards.

but Taylor did exactly that, including a note saying: "Thanks for playing too long and too loud on the Flatts tour. I sincerely appreciate it. Taylor."

Throughout 2007 and 2008, Taylor released several more singles including 'Teardrops on My Guitar', 'Our Song', 'Picture to Burn', and 'Should've Said No'. Taylor saw immense chart success and both 'Our Song' and 'Should've Said No' reached the top spot on *Billboard*'s Hot Country Songs. The success of 'Our Song' led to Taylor becoming the youngest person to single-handedly write and sing a number one song on the chart. To promote the album, Taylor joined other country musicians on their tours between 2006 and 2007, including Brad Paisley, George Strait, and Tim McGraw and Faith Hill on their joint tour. In 2008, she supported Rascal Flatts again when they went on tour.

Taylor's album was popular with critics, who praised her songwriting ability and lauded the album's maturity. For example, *Country Weekly*'s Chris Neal spoke of Taylor's "honesty,

With hard worth and determination, Taylor made her dream of becoming a musician come true.

A 16-year-old Taylor at the Thanksgiving Day NFL game where she sang 'The Star-Spangled Banner', November 2006.

A portrait of Taylor at the 2007 Country Music Awards, where she won the Horizon Award that honours new artists.

Images/Getty

> "My parents raised me to never feel like I was entitled to success. That you have to work for it. You have to work so hard for it.
>
> Taylor Swift

Taylor pictured with Scott Borchetta (founder of Big Machine Records) in 2006.

On stage at the Academy of Country Music Awards All-Star Jam in May 2007.

Images: Getty

A portrait of Taylor taken at the 2006 CMT Music Awards in Nashville, Tennessee.

In the first few years of her career, Taylor sang the national anthem at several sports events. She is pictured at the 2008 World Series in Philadelphia.

Taylor toured with other artists in 2006-2007 and performed at awards ceremonies to promote her debut album.

Images: Getty

In her early country music days, nobody could have anticipated the incredible heights Taylor would reach with the career she was carving out for herself.

CHAPTER 2

Taylor's Evolution

Known for her fresh ideas, fans get to see a different side to Taylor with each new album

Over the course of a career spanning nine studio albums, six EPs, two re-recorded albums, 14 compilations and three live albums, Taylor's music has evolved from her early country days, through to pop, and more recently to indie and folk. Taylor stands as one of the most dynamic musicians in the industry today, known for pushing boundaries and surprising fans with her fresh ideas. Let's explore her artistic evolution…

Taylor's country beginnings

Taylor's interest in music was strengthened during her visits to Nashville, Tennessee, a major centre for not only the genre itself, but the music industry as a whole. It was during those visits that she discovered her passion for pursuing a career in country music.

"When I was 10, or younger than that, even, I would watch these biographies on Faith Hill or the Dixie Chicks or Shania Twain or LeAnn Rimes," Taylor told *Entertainment Weekly*, "And the thing I kept hearing was that they had to go to Nashville."

Following her dream wasn't always smooth sailing, however. A young Taylor would face a lot of rejection in those first attempts. "I took my demo CDs of karaoke songs, where I sound like a chipmunk," she explained. "I knocked on doors up and down Music Row. I would say, 'Hi, I'm Taylor. I'm 11; I want a record deal. Call me'."

Those unsuccessful pitches made Taylor realise that singing covers would not be enough to get her noticed. A few years later – after she had learned the guitar and ▶▶

Taylor pictured at her first MTV Video Music Awards in 2008 (left) and more recently in 2022 (right).

MUSIC TELEVI

Images: Getty

Taylor pictured with her country music idols Faith Hill (left) and Tim McGraw (right).

Rehearsing for a performance at the 42nd Academy of Country Music Awards in May 2007.

started writing her own songs – she was finally turning heads in Nashville and had established working relationships with renowned Music Row songwriters. Taylor eventually signed with Big Machine Records at the age of 15, and began working on her first record.

Taylor's self-titled debut album, released in 2006, featured an authentic Taylor-certified country sound. Taylor is first and foremost a storyteller, and the album gave fans the chance to join her on a journey through her observations of romantic relationships and friendships, giving fans a relatable teenage perspective on heartbreak and love. This distinguished her from many country singers at the time, and enabled her to explore a more Nashville country sound. In fact, in 2009, she told *Variety* "I don't sing about tractors and hay bales and things like that, because that's not really the way that I grew up."

Taylor's skills for songwriting were at the forefront of tracks such as 'Teardrops on My Guitar', which was her first top-15 entry on the *Billboard* Hot 100. The track remains one of her most iconic songs to date, and was inspired by her love for a classmate who didn't feel the same way. On 'Picture to Burn', Taylor's lyrics depicted the protagonist burning a photograph of an ex-boyfriend. On 'Tied Together with a Smile', the lyrics describe a girl who is struggling with her own mental health, and was written the same day Taylor found out one of her best friends had an eating disorder. Later, Taylor said, "I always thought that one of the biggest overlooked problems American girls face is insecurity." Critics praised the album for her fearless songwriting capabilities too, with *Billboard*'s Jonathan Bradley saying Taylor had captured emotions with "details… so sharp at so small a scale."

Two years later, Taylor released her follow-up album, *Fearless*. On her second studio album, she began to fuse pop elements with her brand of country music, particularly on the album's biggest singles such as 'Love Story' and 'You Belong with Me'. Of course, *Fearless* also featured a video for 'You Belong with Me', which inspired a plethora of internet memes. On *Fearless*, Taylor lived up to the album's name, with a more fun and unbridled sound. On her self-titled debut, unrequited love meant she was shedding 'Teardrops on My Guitar'. *Fearless* was an opportunity for her to confidently declare that if her love interest didn't love her back, then he was making the wrong decision.

Taylor's pop transition

While Taylor has previously described her fifth album *1989* as her "first documented official pop album," some of her previous records already introduced pop elements to her sound, such as

Fearless. Taylor's third album, *Speak Now*, released in 2010, continued to evolve her sound, with infusions of pop and even folk. On *Speak Now*, Taylor wrote and co-produced every song, and it is the only album on which she is given sole songwriting credits.

In an online video chat, Taylor said, "I wrote all the songs myself for this record," as reported by *CMT*. She continued, saying, "It didn't really happen on purpose. It just sort of happened that way. I'd get my best ideas at 3am in Arkansas and didn't have a co-writer around and I'd just finish it. And that would happen again in New York; that would happen again in Boston; that would happen again in Nashville." ▶▶

Taylor at the Grammy Awards in December 2007, where she was nominated for Best New Artist.

Taylor performing a selection of tracks from *Red* in London, November 2012.

Taylor's fourth album, *Red*, pushed her music further into the realm of pop.

Lyrics were at the forefront of *Speak Now*, and arguably one of the album's highlights was 'Back to December', which was a unique song for Taylor as it was not only a breakup ballad, but one that featured introspection and reflection, and an apology. It showed how mature Taylor's lyrics had become, and how her ability to tell a story had evolved since her teenage years.

In 2012, Taylor released her fourth studio album, *Red*, which pushed her music further into the realm of pop. The album's singles, including 'I Knew You Were Trouble' and 'We Are Never Ever Getting Back Together', enabled Taylor to experiment more with a pop sound, while continuing with her roots on songs such as 'All Too Well'. By the time *Red* was released, Taylor's private life had sparked a fan and media frenzy and was firmly on public record. Rather than try to hold on to her privacy, Taylor allowed her celebrity status to frame the record, leading to her writing some of her most fun tracks to date.

Her fifth studio album, *1989*, released in 2014, was full of pop and a more modern sound. The album's title paid homage to her birth year, and, interestingly, it acted as almost a rebirth for her music. It marked an exciting shift for her music, transitioning fully to pop, creating some of her most iconic tracks, including 'Blank Space' and 'Shake It Off'. Similarly to *Red*, *1989* saw Taylor address the way the media portrayed her personal life, poking fun at the sensationalism. This could not be more apparent than on 'Blank Space', which made fun of the sexist way her personal life ▶▶

On stage during the Speak Now World Tour in November 2011. Taylor played more than 100 shows at sold-out stadiums and arenas on the tour.

Images: Getty

29

was focused on, and was supported by a cinematic music video that featured Taylor as the 'crazy villain'. According to Joseph Kahn, who directed the clip, Taylor approached him with "a video addressing this concept of, if she has so many boys breaking up with her maybe the problem isn't the boy, maybe the problem is her."

1989 also includes the quickest song Taylor has ever written, which she confirmed in *Vogue*'s '73 Questions'. She told the interviewer that 'Blank Space' took the least amount of time to write "'cause [she'd] written a lot of the lines down already in the year preceding the session." She also confirmed that 'All Too Well', from her album *Red*, took the longest to write, explaining, "It's a really emotional song, I kept putting it down for months on end."

Three years later, her sixth studio album, *reputation*, arrived. Like the two records before, *reputation* was Taylor's way of hitting back at tabloid scrutiny. Prior to the album's release, and following several highly publicised disputes with fellow celebrities, she had avoided social media and the press, and lived a more private life. *reputation* was Taylor's powerful response to sensationalised media gossip and criticism. She also did not promote the album on a press tour, and later described the album as a "defence mechanism."

reputation was Taylor's fourth consecutive album to debut at the number one spot on the US *Billboard* 200, and the album became the world's best-selling album by a female artist. Sonically, *reputation* was firmly in the realm of pop, with strong synths and a clear departure from her earlier country sound. Its lead single, 'Look What You Made Me Do', marked a

Taylor poses with her AMA trophies in November 2013, including the award for Favorite Country Album for *Red*.

Taylor Swift's Reputation Stadium Tour in 2018 was her most successful tour to date.

darker feel for Taylor's music in a fierce return after her public hiatus, and was supported by a satirical music video that featured Taylor in several different scenarios designed to bash the public narrative about her. She said that the premise was rooted in the idea that, "If everything you write about me was true, this is how ridiculous it would look." *reputation* was Taylor's final album under her 12-year contract with Big Machine Records, and she signed a new contract with Universal Music Group in November 2018.

Her next record, *Lover*, was her last pop album before she committed to more experimentation with folk music. All 18 of the album's songs charted on the *Billboard* Hot 100 the same week, which saw Taylor set a new record for the most simultaneous entries by a woman in the charts. The album's lead single 'ME!', which featured Panic! At The Disco's Brendon Urie, is a bubblegum pop duet, and even features a marching band drumline. The album also included standout tracks such as 'You Need to Calm Down', which saw Taylor address internet trolls and homophobes in a video featuring LGBTQ+ icons including Hayley Kiyoko, Ellen DeGeneres and the Fab Five from Netflix's ▶▶

Taylor rocks a retro look in a performance on the 1989 World Tour, November 2015.

Images Getty

For 2020's folklore and evermore, Taylor embraced a more mellow, folk sound. This new direction received great critical acclaim.

The 'Taylor's Versions' of *Fearless* (April 2021) and *Red* (November 2021) topped the charts and broke records.

At the VMAs in August 2022, Taylor announced her 10th studio album, *Midnights*.

Queer Eye. In a pinch-me moment, after years of citing The Chicks as an influence, *Lover* saw Taylor collaborate with them on 'Soon You'll Get Better'.

A new indie & folk sound

After *Lover*, Taylor surprised fans with two albums: *folklore* and *evermore*. *folklore*, released in July 2020, was conceived by Taylor in quarantine during the Covid-19 pandemic, and saw her blend a more mellow sound with indie folk and alternative melodies. It saw Taylor break away from both her country and pop days, embarking on an even more mature journey that enabled her to use a multitude of themes to tell a story, including romanticism, nostalgia and melancholia. The album's introspective nature led to widespread critical acclaim, and *folklore* is widely regarded as Taylor's best album to date, with some critics even referring to it as pioneering.

Just a few months later, in December 2020, Taylor released her follow-up album, *evermore*. Like *folklore*, it was a surprise album, announced just hours before its release. She dubbed both lockdown records as 'sister albums', and *evermore* continued with that same folk-pop and indie style. Excitingly, *evermore* featured guest vocals from Bon Iver, Haim and The National, and was also well-received by critics who saw it as a brilliant expansion on the experimentation Taylor used on *folklore*.

In 2021, Taylor released the first albums of her highly anticipated re-recording project: *Fearless (Taylor's Version)* in April and *Red (Taylor's Version)* in November. Critics and fans alike praised Taylor's faithful recreations of the beloved classic tracks, and welcomed the addition of bonus material in the form of previously unreleased 'From the Vault' tracks. In particular, at ten minutes and 13 seconds, the new, unabridged 'All Too Well (10 Minute Version)' broke the Guinness World Record for the Longest Song to Reach No. 1 on the *Billboard* Hot 100.

Taylor also wrote and directed a short film based on 'All Too Well (10 Minute Version)', for which she won Video of the Year at the MTV VMAs in August 2022. During her acceptance speech, she made the surprise announcement that her tenth studio album, *Midnights*, will be released in October. At the time of writing, there is much speculation regarding the genre of the album and whether it will continue the indie sounds of *folklore* and *evermore*, or perhaps something different altogether.

Taylor is widely regarded as one of the greatest songwriters and musical storytellers. She has continuously used her music as a device to control her own narrative, and empower fans to address their own heartbreaks, romances and trials and tribulations. Never afraid of reinvention, fans are always excited to hear what Taylor will create next.

"
I love everyone who's inspired me to write a song, whether you know it or not.

Taylor's album liner notes for her debut record, 2006
"

Taylor performing at Stagecoach, California's Country Music Festival in May 2008.

On stage in New York City during the Fearless Tour at Madison Square Garden, August 2009.

To me, fearless is living in spite of those things that scare you to death.

Taylor's album liner notes for *Fearless*, 2008

Images: Getty

35

Sharing the love with the crowd in Rotterdam, Netherlands, during the Speak Now World Tour in March 2011.

" These songs are made up of words I didn't say when the moment was right in front of me.

Taylor's album liner notes for *Speak Now*, 2010 "

> **My experiences in love have taught me difficult lessons, especially my experiences with crazy love. The red relationships.**
>
> Taylor's album liner notes for *Red*, 2012

Performing on The Red Tour at the Staples Center in Los Angeles, in August 2013.

Taylor performs in Singapore during the 1989 World Tour in November 2015.

"I've told you my stories for years now. Some have been about coming of age. Some have been about coming undone. This is a story about coming into your own, and as a result... coming alive.

Taylor's album liner notes for *1989*, 2014

> We think we know someone, but the truth is that we only know the version of them that they have chosen to show us.
>
> Taylor's album liner notes for *reputation*, 2017

Taylor Swift's Reputation Stadium Tour broke many records, becoming the third highest-grossing concert tour of all time by a female artist (behind Madonna and P!nk).

ME!

This album is
a love letter to
love itself.

Taylor's album liner
notes for *Lover*, 2019

Taylor poses with a
butterfly mural in
Nashville, Tennessee, to
promote *Lover* in April
2019. Her Lover Fest tour,
planned for 2020, was
unfortunately cancelled

In isolation my imagination has run wild and this album is the result, a collection of songs and stories that flowed like a stream of consciousness.

Taylor's personal essay about *folklore*, July 2020

Taylor performed a medley of songs from *folklore* and *evermore* on an ethereal stage set at the Grammys in March 2021.

Images: Alamy, Getty

41

The release of *evermore*, less than five months after *folklore*, broke the record for the shortest gap between new No. 1 albums on the US Billboard 200 chart.

We just couldn't stop writing songs... I loved the escapism I found in these imaginary / not imaginary tales.

Taylor's personal essay about *evermore*, December 2020

Taylor at the VMAs in August 2022, where she announced her 10th studio album, *Midnights*.

> This is a collection of music written in the middle of the night, a journey through terrors and sweet dreams.
>
> Taylor's announcement message for *Midnights*, 2022

Change Maker

It's no secret that Taylor has been subtle about many of her political views, choosing instead to quietly support a range of worthy causes

For most of her career, Taylor has steered clear from taking a public stand when it comes to politics. Until recently, she chose to support causes in a more discreet way. However, she is well known for her charity work, and was even ranked at number one on the 'Gone Good' list by DoSomething, a global non-profit organisation that motivates young people to make a positive change. So what exactly makes Taylor such a force for good?

Taylor's generosity

Throughout her career, Taylor has been a strong advocate for supporting the amazing work done by charities and non-profit organisations. Taylor is regarded as one of the most charitable celebrities, and it's obvious why. While she doesn't shout about her various charitable actions, her support and donations have frequently been picked up by the press.

Taylor has donated several items, such as guitars, to charity auctions in aid of the UNICEF Tap Project, the Elton John AIDS Foundation and MusiCares, to name a few. She's worked with various organisations including the Make-A-Wish Foundation and Habitat for Humanity, and also encouraged young people to volunteer in their local communities as part of Global Youth Service Day.

In 2008, the same year she released *Fearless*, Taylor donated $100,000 to the Red Cross to support those affected by the Iowa flood, which lasted for ▶▶

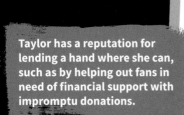

Taylor has a reputation for lending a hand where she can, such as by helping out fans in need of financial support with impromptu donations.

Images: Getty

In her early career, Taylor would often show her love and appreciation for her fans with the hand heart gesture.

> As Taylor's success has grown, so have the amounts she has donated.

several weeks between June and July 2008 and caused $6 billion worth of property damage.

As her success has grown, so have the amounts she has donated. In 2010, she donated $500,000 to the relief effort following the Tennessee floods in May that year, and the following year, after receiving the Academy of Country Music's Entertainer of the Year award, she donated $25,000 to St Jude Children's Research Hospital, based in Tennessee.

In 2014, Taylor donated $100,000 to the V Foundation for Cancer Research and $50,000 to the Children's Hospital of Philadelphia. In 2016, she gave a whopping $1 million to the Louisiana flood relief efforts and $100,000 to the Dolly Parton Fire Fund. The following year, she donated to the Houston Food Bank after the city suffered damage from Hurricane Harvey. More recently, she also gave $1 million to relief efforts following the Tennessee tornado in 2020.

Taylor has performed at several charity relief events, including Sydney's Sound Relief concert, in aid of those affected by the February 2009 Victorian bushfires. She also contributed to the 2010 live

First Lady Michelle Obama presents Taylor with the Big Help award at Nickelodeon's Kids' Choice Awards in March 2012.

Taylor performing for the *One World* special during the Covid-19 pandemic lockdowns.

album *Hope for Haiti Now* with her song 'Breathless', which was released to help victims of the 2010 Haiti earthquake. After the 2011 Super Outbreak, which saw more than 175 tornadoes affect areas across the US, Taylor used a dress rehearsal of her Speak Now Tour as a benefit concert for victims of those disasters.

In 2012, she took part in the Stand Up to Cancer telethon and performed 'Ronan', which she wrote in memory of a four-year-old boy who died of neuroblastoma, a type of cancer that affects certain types of nerve tissue. All proceeds from the sales of the song were donated to cancer-related charities.

During the Covid-19 pandemic, Taylor has supported several causes across the world. For example, she donated to the World Health Organization (WHO) and Feeding America, and supported the UK's NHS by offering to donate one of her signed guitars as part of an auction to raise money for the health service. For the *One World: Together* ▷▷

Images: Getty, Alamy

In recent years, Taylor has started bringing attention to social and political issues in her acceptance speeches.

at Home television special, she performed in aid of the WHO's Covid-19 Solidarity Response Fund.

Her passion for charity work has led her to receive a number of accolades, including the 'Star of Compassion', given to her by the Tennessee Disaster Services, The Big Help Award from the Nickelodeon Kids' Choice Awards for her "dedication to helping others" and "inspiring others through action," and the Ripple of Hope Award for her "dedication to advocacy at such a young age."

Giving back to her fans

Taylor publicly supports both big and small causes, but also takes an interest in helping her loyal fan base. She is known for making frequent donations to fans' GoFundMe pages, helping in any way she can from contributing to medical bills to paying towards college funds.

Taylor usually donates in a subtle way, with many of her contributions only becoming public when the recipient chooses to speak about it. Some earlier examples of Taylor's generosity include her sending a fan $1,989 to help her start paying her student loan debt in January 2015, and giving $10,000 three years later to a boy with autism, so his family could pay for him to own a service dog.

In 2019, she paid for a fan battling cancer to cover their medical expenses. 16-year-old Trinity Foster was diagnosed with stage four osteosarcoma, which had spread to her lung. Taylor donated $10,000 to her GoFundMe page, which she had launched to pay for her medical bills. She left a note saying, "I saw photos of your album release ▶▶

Images: Getty,

Taylor takes photos with fans at the MTV Video Music Awards in August 2019.

49

Performing with Jon Bon Jovi and Prince William at the Winter Whites Gala in aid of the youth homelessness charity Centrepoint, November 2013.

party that you did in your hospital room and wanted to say thank you for being so kind and supportive!"

The Covid-19 pandemic has put significant financial strain on people across the world. Taylor has stepped up over the last two years, contributing money to a range of funds, and sending gifts to her fans. For example, in April 2021, healthcare worker Britta Thomason revealed that Taylor had sent her a care package full of merch, 'cosy clothes' and self-care items, as well as a note to say thank you for working on the front line during the pandemic. Taylor and her mother, Andrea, also helped Vickie Quarles, a mother of five daughters, reach her GoFundMe goal so that she could support her family after her husband died of Covid-19 the week before Christmas.

Contributions by Taylor to her fans also include a donation of around £10,000 to two mothers who were struggling during the Covid-19 pandemic. She sent money to Nikki Cornwell from Nashville who had rent arrears of $5,000 after being unable to work while ill with coronavirus. Taylor also sent money to Shelbie Selewski from Michigan who lost her job at the start of the pandemic and was due to be evicted.

She surprised Emerson Weber, an 11-year-old fan from South Dakota, with a care package after Weber had been giving back to postal workers during the pandemic. Taylor also quietly gave financial support to Grimey's New & Preloved Music, a Nashville record shop that had been forced to shut amid the pandemic. They told *Rolling Stone* that Taylor had paid staff salaries and healthcare for three months.

Politics & activism

It's no secret that Taylor has kept relatively quiet about her political views for some time now. In

Taylor performing at the BBC's Children in Need fundraising event in November 2009.

In 2017, Taylor donated $250,000 towards fellow singer Kesha's legal battle against producer Dr Luke.

fact, it wasn't until 2018 that she began to be more vocal on political issues. That year, she endorsed the Senate candidate for Tennessee, the Democrat Phil Bredesen. Since then, she has been a fierce public supporter of a number of political viewpoints.

In 2008, she joined celebrities for a public service announcement (PSA) to raise awareness of the murder of gay teenager Lawrence King, who was shot in February that year. The PSA was created for LOGOonline.com, and Taylor appeared in the video, saying, "Don't close your eyes to discrimination." In 2009, she acknowledged that she was a supporter of Barack Obama's successful bid to be elected as America's first Black president. She told *Rolling Stone*, "I've never seen this country so happy about a political decision in my entire time of being alive."

However, she was notably quiet for years following a public feud with Kanye West and his former wife, Kim Kardashian, which escalated in July 2016. It wasn't until a couple of years later, ▶▶

Images: Getty, Alamy

51

Taylor's influence was tangible... The sudden surge in voter registrations was described as the 'Swift Lift'.

in 2018, when she became more vocal with her public support of political issues and causes.

That year, she posted on Instagram in support of March For Our Lives, confirming that she had made a donation to the campaign. She wrote: "I'm so moved by the Parkland High School students, faculty, by all families and friends of victims who have spoken out, trying to prevent this from happening again."

She also endorsed political figures for the first time, voicing support for Phil Bredesen for Senate and Jim Cooper for House of Representatives. She took to Instagram to write: "In the past I've been reluctant to publicly voice my political opinions, but due to several events in my life and in the world in the past two years, I feel very differently about that now […] I believe in the fight for LGBTQ rights, and that

any form of discrimination based on sexual orientation or gender is WRONG. I believe that the systemic racism we still see in this country towards people of color is terrifying, sickening and prevalent."

It was the first time Taylor had officially confirmed she was a Democrat, and Taylor's influence was tangible. 160,000 people registered to vote within 48 hours of Taylor's post in October (compared to fewer than 57,000 registrations in the whole of August). Political commentators described the sudden surge in voter registrations as the 'Swift Lift'.

Taylor calls for a response to the Equality Act petition during her speech at the MTV VMAs in 2019.

As a public figure, Taylor's actions and words can have a significant influence on her fanbase.

CHANGE MAKER

In June 2019, Taylor also revealed that she had written to her senator, asking them to support the Equality Act, and created a petition on Change.org. She encouraged her followers to do the same and said she would keep track of their letters with the hashtag #lettertomysenator. Later that month, she released her music video for 'You Need to Calm Down', a major statement in favour of LGBTQ+ liberation. The music video featured several famous members of the LGBTQ+ community including Hayley Kiyoko and Ellen DeGeneres, and she sang the lyrics, "You are somebody that we don't know / But you're comin' at my friends like a missile / Why are you mad? / When you could be GLAAD?"

In August 2019, she called Trump's presidency an "autocracy", adding, "We're a democracy – at least, we're supposed to be – where you're allowed to disagree, dissent, debate." She also called out the White House during her VMAs speech after winning video of the year for 'You Need to Calm Down'.

She said, "At the end of this video, there was a petition and there still is a petition for the Equality Act, which basically just says we all deserve equal rights under the law. I want to thank everyone who signed that petition because it now has a half a million signatures, which is five times the amount that it would need to warrant a response from the White House." She then looked at her wrist, pointing to an imaginary watch to highlight the fact that the government's response on the matter was well overdue.

Taylor has consistently been one of the most generous celebrities in the business. It has taken her years to gain the confidence to speak publicly about the issues that matter to her, but Taylor is learning how powerful her voice can be as a force for positive change.

The music video and 2019 VMA performance (pictured) of 'You Need to Calm Down' featured cameos by many celebrities from the LGBTQ+ community.

Images: Getty

53

> No matter what happens in life, be good to people. Being good to people is a wonderful legacy to leave behind.
>
> Taylor Swift

Taylor has always been incredibly generous with her fans, spending time with them and even providing financial support for those in need.

Image: Getty

After a long legal battle, Taylor eventually won her case against former DJ David Mueller in August 2017.

MUELLER V. SWIFT

PUBLIC COURTROOM VIEWING ACCESS LINE

STARTS HERE 6AM

"MY HOPE IS TO HELP THOSE WHOSE VOICES SHOULD ALSO BE HEARD."

TAYLOR GAVE A STATEMENT AFTER HER VICTORY IN HER CASE AGAINST DAVID MUELLER. SHE ALSO PLEDGED TO DONATE TO CHARITIES THAT SUPPORT OTHER VICTIMS OF SEXUAL ASSAULT

FEARLESS

Messages of support for Taylor were displayed in the windows of a building across from the courthouse where the trial took place.

PEOPLE THROW ROCKS AT THINGS THAT SHINE

#BlankSpaceForTaylor

57

"I HAVE WATCHED AS WOMEN IN THIS INDUSTRY ARE CRITICIZED AND MEASURED UP TO EACH OTHER AND PICKED AT FOR THEIR BODIES, THEIR ROMANTIC LIVES, THEIR FASHION... OR HAVE YOU EVER HEARD SOMEONE SAY ABOUT A MALE ARTIST, 'I REALLY LIKE HIS SONGS BUT I DON'T KNOW WHAT IT IS, THERE'S JUST SOMETHING ABOUT HIM I DON'T LIKE'? NO! THAT CRITICISM IS RESERVED FOR US!"

TAYLOR CALLED OUT DOUBLE STANDARDS IN THE MUSIC INDUSTRY DURING HER ACCEPTANCE SPEECH AT THE 2019 BILLBOARD WOMEN IN MUSIC EVENT

"
I want to thank everyone who signed that petition because it now has half a million signatures, which is five times the amount it would need to warrant a response from the White House...

Taylor called out the government for not responding to the Equality Act petition at the 2019 MTV VMAs
"

Taylor posing with singer and choreographer Todrick Hall backstage at *Kinky Boots* on Broadway. The pair are close friends, and Todrick has helped Taylor realise her voice can be a powerful instrument for positive change as an ally of the LGBTQ+ community.

Images: Getty

Love, heartache & Her Triple-Platinum Life

d White d Worn All Over
Dresses, Pants, Trench Coats

THE PEOPLE ISSUE '09

Rolling Stone

Issue 1218
September 25, 2014
$4.99

The New Life of Taylor Swift

FALL PREVIEW

U2
Kendrick Lamar
Foo Fighters
Nicki Minaj
Stevie Nicks
Kanye West
Jackson Browne
Weezer
Charli XCX

CHINA & GLOBAL WARMING

The Fight to Rein in the World's Biggest Polluter

PLUS

ROBERT PLANT
ANDRÉ 3000
BILL HADER
APHEX TWIN
NICK CAVE

750 Spring Looks For YOU

100 Best Beauty Tricks Of 2014
Gorgeous hair & skin all year

Since her teens, Taylor's personal life has been the subject of intense media speculation and scrutiny.

Getting Personal

With global fame comes intense media attention on every aspect of your life, but Taylor has had to endure a great deal more than most...

Like any celebrity, Taylor's personal life has been the subject of media scrutiny. However, in her case, that is a bit of an understatement: a media frenzy over a string of public feuds with other artists, as well as sexist coverage of her relationship history, led the singer to take a much-needed break from public life.

Taylor's relationships

Taylor has endured widespread public interest in her dating life, particularly as she regularly uses it for inspiration for her songwriting. One of her most high-profile relationships was with fellow singer Harry Styles, whom she began dating from November 2012 until January 2013. While their relationship was short lived, it is believed that her song 'Out of the Woods' is about Styles, with many stating their relationship ended badly.

At her performance at the Grammy Museum, she told the audience about the song's inspiration, saying, "The number one feeling I felt in the whole relationship was anxiety, because it felt very fragile, it felt very tentative. And it always felt like, 'OK, what's the next roadblock?'" In return, some of Styles' fans believe his track 'Two Ghosts' is about Taylor, and during a 2017 interview on BBC Radio 1, he was asked if this was the case, responding with, "I think it's pretty self-explanatory."

A few years before her relationship with Styles, she began dating fellow musician Joe Jonas of the Jonas Brothers. Taylor and Jonas dated from July to October ▶▶

Joe Jonas

Tom Hiddleston

Calvin Harris

Taylor Lautner

Taylor has had high-profile boyfriends in the past, but has found a happy balance with British actor Joe Alwyn (right) as the pair have managed to keep their relationship private.

Joe Alwyn

Harry Styles

2008, and in true Noughties-style, their break-up caused a lot of drama. During an interview on *Ellen*, she confirmed that he had broken up with her "over the phone," saying, "When I find that person who is right for me, he'll be wonderful, and when I look at that person, I'm not even gonna be able to remember the boy who broke up with me over the phone in 25 seconds when I was 18."

Her breakup with Jonas provided the inspiration for her song, 'Forever and Always', which appeared on her second studio album, *Fearless*. The song included jabs at Jonas for his behaviour, with Taylor singing, "Was I out of line? / Did I say something way too honest, made you run and hide / Like a scared little boy."

A year later, she appeared on *Saturday Night Live* and delivered her opening monologue, poking fun at the breakup: "You might think I'd bring up Joe, that guy who broke up with me on the phone. But I'm not going to mention him in my monologue. Hey, Joe! I'm doing real well and I'm hosting *SNL* – but I'm not going to write about that in my monologue."

While filming the romantic comedy film *Valentine's Day*, Taylor began dating *Twilight* actor, and fellow cast member, Taylor Lautner, during autumn 2009. The pair shared several scenes together, and she allegedly wrote 'Back to December', which appears on her third studio album, *Speak Now*, about Lautner. Adding to the frequent criticism levied at Taylor for her choice to write songs about her love life, Lautner was asked what he thought of the song in 2016, answering with, "That's what she does."

She began another high-profile relationship late that year, dating singer John Mayer between December 2009 and February 2010. Her song 'Dear John', which appeared on *Speak Now*, explored their relationship, and Mayer complained about the track in an interview with *Rolling Stone*, telling the publication he was "really humiliated." He added, "I ▶▶

Images: Getty, Alamy

> Allegedly, many songs on Taylor's fourth studio album, *Red*, were inspired by Jake Gyllenhaal.

will say as a songwriter that I think it's kind of cheap songwriting. I know she's the biggest thing in the world, and I'm not trying to sink anybody's ship, but I think it's abusing your talent to rub your hands together and go, 'Wait till he gets a load of this!' That's bulls***."

Afterwards, Taylor dated actor Jake Gyllenhaal (*Donnie Darko, The Day After Tomorrow, Nightcrawler*) between October 2010 and January 2011. Reportedly, the relationship came to an abrupt ending; a source told *Us Weekly*, which had originally broken the story of their relationship, that Taylor felt "really burned by him." Allegedly, many songs on her fourth studio album, *Red*, were inspired by Gyllenhaal. While Taylor didn't confirm this, she did tell *New York Magazine* that the man in question said listening to *Red* "was like going through a photo album."

Some years later, Taylor released a re-recorded version of *Red*, as well as a short film for her single 'All Too Well'. It reignited rumours that Gyllenhaal provided inspiration for the song, and the lyrics "And I left my scarf there at your sister's house / And you've still got it in your drawer even now" sent fans into a frenzy all over again. Legendary artist Dionne Warwick, who is known for her witty, tongue-in-cheek moments online, tweeted "If that young man has Taylor's scarf he should return it", following it with "It does not belong to you. Box it up and I will pay the cost of postage, Jake."

Between February 2015 and May 2016, Taylor dated Scottish DJ and producer Calvin Harris. Two months after they celebrated their one-year anniversary, *People* reported that Harris had ended the relationship. Amid much media speculation regarding the cause of the breakup, Harris tweeted: "The only truth here is that a relationship came to an end & what remains is a huge amount of love and respect". ▶▶

Taylor with fellow singer and BFF Selena Gomez.

Taylor poses with some of her 'squad' of famous friends at the MTV VMAs in August 2015. L-R: Martha Hunt, Hailee Steinfeld, Cara Delevingne, Selena Gomez, Taylor, Serayah McNeill, Lily Aldridge, Gigi Hadid.

Taylor with her friend Abigail Anderson at the Grammy Awards in February 2015. They have been friends since Taylor was 15.

At the iHeartRadio Jingle Ball in 2019, Taylor was presented with a giant cake for her 30th birthday, complete with decorations of her beloved pet cats.

Taylor dated actor Tom Hiddleston (*Thor, War Horse, High Rise*) for several months between May and September 2016, and the pair were first spotted dancing together at the Met Gala. *The Sun* published pictures of them kissing in Rhode Island, with many believing the images were staged. Things escalated when they were seen dancing together at a Selena Gomez concert, and Hiddleston was photographed wearing an 'I HEART TS' top. However, they broke up in September 2016, after a source told the *Daily Mail* that Taylor felt "uncomfortable" with "Tom's need for their relationship to be so public so quickly."

Fast forward to now, and Taylor has found happiness in her relationship with actor Joe Alwyn (*Operation Finale, The Favourite, Harriet*). The pair reportedly met in 2016, but *The Sun* broke the news of their relationship, saying Taylor had been staying, in disguise, in London. Since then, paparazzi have caught glimpses of their blossoming romance, including snapping photos of them at the premiere of Alwyn's film *The Favourite*, and at the BAFTAs in 2019. Alwyn also collaborated with Taylor on her 2020 albums *folklore* and *evermore*, with a co-writing credit under the name William Bowery.

Taylor & the media

Throughout her career, Taylor has been regarded as polite and open by journalists, who praise her willingness to 'play along' during interviews. In fact, J Freedom du Lac of *The Washington Post* once called her a "media darling" and "a reporter's dream." In the world of fashion journalism, *Vogue* named her an Icon of American Style in 2011, and she topped *People*'s best-dressed list in 2014.

Rather aptly, however, she told the interviewer during a 73 Questions video for *Vogue* that she would tell her 19-year-old self: "Hey, you're going to date just like a normal 20-something should be allowed to, but you're going to be a national lightning rod for slut-shaming." Sexist coverage of Taylor's personal life can be traced as far back as 2013, when Taylor was in her early-20s, and *The New York Times* questioned whether she was having a "quarter-life crisis," stating her "dating history has begun to stir what feels like the beginning of a backlash." Following the release of *1989*, *Rolling Stone* churned out extensive news coverage of Taylor after stating "everything [Taylor] did was a story."

Taylor has used her music to criticise the media frenzy surrounding her personal life. For example, her 2014 track 'Blank Space' saw her parody the stereotypes the media had used to categorise her as 'crazy', 'manipulative' and 'seductive'. She also explored themes of gaslighting and double standards on her songs 'mad woman' and 'The Man', respectively.

When *CBS* journalist Tracy Smith asked her, "Why sing to the haters?" she replied, defiantly, with, "Well, when they stop coming for me, I will stop singing to them." ▶▶

Taylor and her childhood friend Britany Maack at the Grammy Gala in 2014. Taylor was Britany's maid of honour at her wedding in 2016.

Images: Getty

Her family & friends

While Taylor's parents are not overly creative themselves, they heavily encouraged her pursuit of a career in music. Her parents both worked in the finance and banking sectors: her mother, Andrea Gardner Swift, was a mutual fund marketing executive, and her father, Scott Kingsley Swift, is a former stockbroker for Merrill. In terms of her heritage, Taylor's paternal great-great-grandfather was an Italian immigrant who owned several businesses in Philadelphia in the 1800s. And, of course, her maternal grandmother, Marjorie Finlay, was an opera singer.

Her younger brother, Austin, is an actor, known for roles in *Live by Night*, *Braking for Whales* and *We Summon the Darkness*. Austin graduated from University of Notre Dame in May 2015, and worked as a photographer for Getty Images on a freelance basis while he was studying. Nowadays, he can be found in Taylor's music videos alongside the siblings' friends.

Taylor surrounds herself with strong female friendships, and in the mid-2010s, her A-list friends became known as the 'squad': a group of famous women that included Cara Delevingne, Selena Gomez, Gigi Hadid and Hailee Steinfeld to name but a few. In fact, they appeared in her video for the remixed version of her song 'Bad Blood', featuring American rapper Kendrick Lamar. The video, set in London, saw an ensemble cast star in a futuristic spy story.

Taylor also has a number of other famous friends, including Ryan Reynolds and Blake Lively, whose daughter can be heard on Taylor's song 'Gorgeous'. She is also close friends with supermodel Martha Hunt (they reportedly met at a Victoria's Secret Fashion Show Taylor performed at in 2014), and Selena Gomez, who told the *Wall Street Journal*: "We both went through s*** at the same time. She taught me a lot about how to be treated at a young age."

She also still keeps in touch with her friends back home. In 2016, *Vogue* reported that Taylor returned to Reading, Pennsylvania, to attend the wedding of her childhood friend, Britany Maack. Taylor was maid of honour, and delivered a beautiful speech, flitting between humour and touching sentimentality, saying, "Real love doesn't mess with your head. Real love just is. Real love just endures. Real love maintains. Real love takes it page by page." Abigail Anderson, another hometown friend, met Taylor when they went to high school together, and even starred in some of Taylor's earlier music videos.

Taylor's pets & interests

Taylor's love for animals is well-known. In an interview with *Vogue* in 2016, she recalled that her mum encouraged her to pursue horseback riding, which Taylor took part in competitively until she was 12 years old. Not only did Taylor star in the infamous 2019 film *Cats*, but she also has three

Taylor's mother and father have always been on her side throughout her career.

Taylor with her brother, Austin, at the Golden Globes after party in January 2014.

pet kitties of her own: Olivia Benson, named after the *Law and Order: Special Victims Unit* character; Meredith Grey, named after the iconic protagonist from *Grey's Anatomy*; and Benjamin Button, who has been part of the family since 2019. She frequently posts funny pictures of her pets on her Instagram, and Olivia Benson was placed higher than Grumpy Cat on the 2018 Pet Rich List (yes, that is a thing).

In her free time, Taylor is known to hang out with her cats, and watch *Friends*, which she has called her favourite show currently not on air. She told *GQ* magazine that it is her favourite thing to watch after performing to crowds of tens of thousands

and meeting her fans. She was also spotted in 2018 in California, where she took a falconry class, and revealed that during the Covid-19 lockdown, she has been watching films, reading and cooking.

Life in the public eye was never going to be easy, especially when you become world famous as a teenager. But Taylor has managed to navigate the madness of media attention better than most. She has kept her feet on the ground through it all, thanks in no small part to the importance she places on her relationships, and the enduring support of her loved ones.

Taylor with her brother, Austin, and mother, Andrea, taking a walk in New York City, 2014.

Taylor pictured with her cat, Olivia Benson, named after the *Law & Order: SVU* character. She has two other cats: Meredith Grey, named after the *Grey's Anatomy* character, and Benjamin Button, named after the character in F Scott Fitzgerald's famous story.

Images: Getty

2008

2011

Taylor and Selena Gomez
have been friends for
more than a decade.
Both artists have faced
the pressures of growing
up in the public eye.

2018

2016

GRA

Images: Getty

75

The Netflix documentary *Miss Americana* gave fans a glimpse into Taylor's closely guarded private life, and revealed her struggles with the intense media scrutiny she faces.

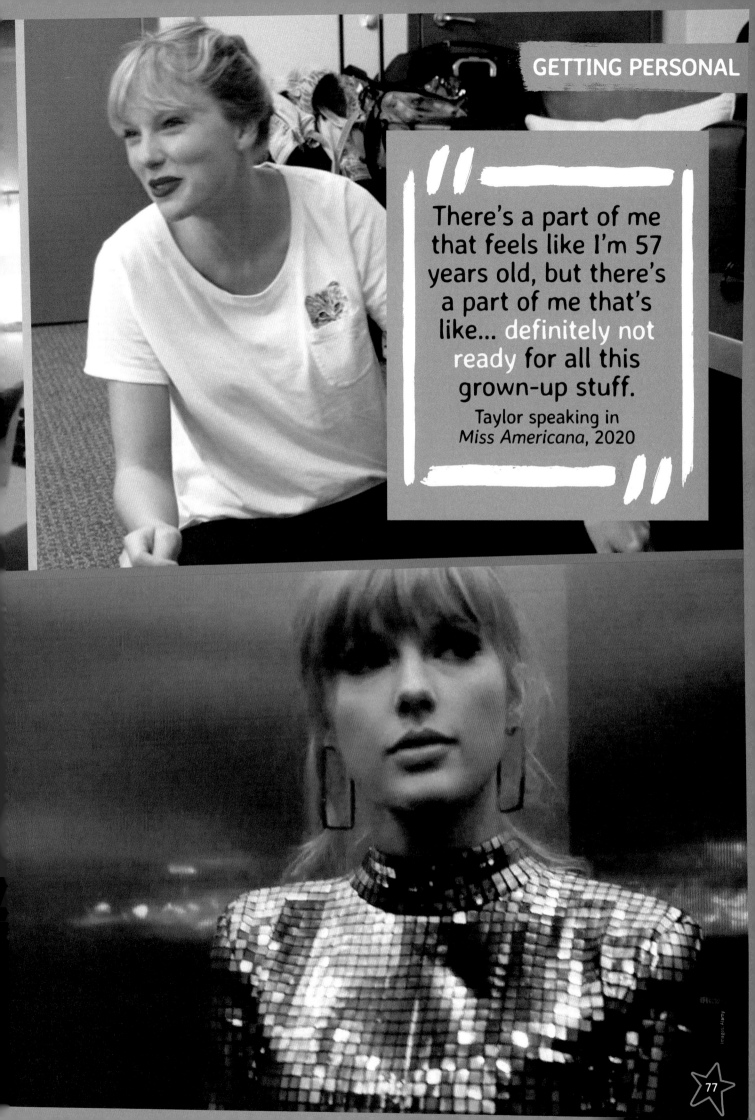

"

There's a part of me that feels like I'm 57 years old, but there's a part of me that's like... definitely not ready for all this grown-up stuff.

Taylor speaking in
Miss Americana, 2020

"

CHAPTER 4

Taylor and Joe have managed to keep their relationship out of the public eye. At the Golden Globes in 2020, they walked the red carpet separately.

78

"I was falling in love with someone who had a wonderfully normal, balanced life... We decided together we wanted our relationship to be private."

Taylor on her relationship with Joe Alwyn

79

Global Icon

Taylor Swift stands as one of the most iconic artists of the 21st century, paving the way for generations to come

Taylor's astonishing career over the past two decades has had a tangible, far-reaching impact on pop music. But not only has she inspired her fellow artists – by taking a stand against injustices that plague the music industry and wider society, Taylor has become a remarkable role model for young people everywhere.

The Swift factor

Taylor is first and foremost an innovator, and one of the most notable musicians when it comes to reinventing her sound. Because of this talent for evolving, she remains one of the key change makers in the modern country music and pop scenes. What's more, many music experts believe her talent also led to her creating a more sustainable interest in country music outside of its American heartland, with music journalist Jody Rosen saying Taylor was the first country artist whose fame reached the world outside of the US.

Taylor has paved the way for younger and future country singers, particularly women. Many critics have noted her influences on albums by fellow female country singers Kacey Musgraves, Maren Morris and Kelsea Ballerini, and an extraordinary number of young musicians have cited Taylor as an influence on their music, including Phoebe Bridgers, Selena Gomez, Billie Eilish, Little Mix, Troye Sivan, Olivia Rodrigo and Hayley Williams.

Rolling Stone cited Taylor as one of the biggest influences on 2010s pop music, ranking her 80th in ▶▶

Taylor Swift's Reputation Stadium Tour became her most successful tour to date, and the highest-grossing US tour in history.

CHAPTER 5

its list of 100 Greatest Country Artists of All Time. In 2020, the publication also ranked her song 'Tim McGraw' at number 11 on its 'The 100 Greatest Debut Singles of All Time' list, stating: "With her first song, Swift immediately showed her Nashville peers she could beat any of them at their own game, acing the classic genre trope of nostalgic country song about how country music is nostalgic."

Retrospective reviews of her debut album have also noted her early songwriting abilities. For example, *Pitchfork* described the record as an honest portrayal of teenage perspectives, distinguishing Taylor from music at the time that involved "weighed down former teen sensations." *Billboard* praised Taylor's ability to capture emotion with "details… so sharp at so small a scale."

Taylor's rise to fame also instigated a phenomenon dubbed the 'Taylor Swift factor', which saw a marked increase in guitar sales to women, while music critic Nick Catucci wrote that the emotion and vulnerability in her lyrics inspired the next generation of pop stars, including Ariana Grande and Billie Eilish. Taylor is also a beacon of millennial popular culture; *Quartz* named her the most important millennial artist, Billy Joel

has said she is the Beatles of her generation, and *Vox* has called her the "millennial Bruce Springsteen."

Critical acclaim

Taylor has received both critical acclaim and acknowledgement at the most prestigious awards ceremonies in the music industry. Her albums have been largely well received by music journalists, with *Rolling Stone*'s Jody Rosen calling Taylor a "songwriting savant" in his review of her sophomore album, *Fearless*. On her third studio album, *Speak Now*, *AllMusic*'s Stephen Thomas Erlewine wrote: "[Swift] writes from the perspective of the moment yet has the skill of a songwriter beyond her years."

Her fourth studio album, *Red*, was also widely praised by critics, and *The Guardian*'s Kate Mossman described it as "one of the finest fantasies pop music has ever constructed." On her fifth studio album, *1989*, *The New York Times* described her as "aiming somewhere even higher, a mode of timelessness that few true pop stars […] even bother aspiring to." More recently, her 2020 sister albums *folklore* and *evermore* received an overwhelmingly positive set of ▶▶

Taylor accepts the Teen Choice Icon Award (complete with photos of her cats!) in August 2019.

Amid the dispute surrounding her back catalogue masters, Taylor used the 2019 AMAs to make a visual statement.

SPEAK NOW
TAYLOR
1989
RED
REPUTATION

"

Taylor's rise to fame also instigated a phenomenon dubbed the 'Taylor Swift factor', which saw a marked increase in guitar sales to women.

"

Taylor accepts the prestigious Woman of the Decade award at the Billboard Women in Music event, December 2019.

Images: Getty

From one legendary songwriter to another: Carole King presented Taylor's Artist of the Decade award (above), and Taylor later inducted Carole into the Rock & Roll Hall of Fame (below).

reviews from critics. *NME*'s Hannah Mylrea described *evermore* as a "freewheeling younger sibling" while *folklore* was the "introspective, romantic older sister."

In terms of awards, Taylor was named Woman of the Decade for the 2010s by *Billboard* and became the first woman to be named Artist of the Decade for the 2010s at the American Music Awards (AMAs). She also received the BRITs Global Icon Award "in recognition of her immense impact on music across the world." As of August 2022, Taylor has won 11 Grammy Awards (including three wins for Album of the Year), 12 Country Music Association Awards, 34 AMAs, 29 *Billboard* Music Awards and an Emmy. She has also received multiple acknowledgements from music organisations such as the Nashville Songwriters Association, the Songwriters Hall of Fame, and the National Music Publishers Association. *Time* magazine has included her on its annual list of the 100 most influential people three times: in 2010, 2015 and 2019. The publication also honoured her as one of the 'Silence Breakers' in 2017 after she spoke about her experience of sexual assault.

Silence breaker

Taylor bravely exposed radio personality David Mueller and successfully sued him for grabbing her bottom in 2013. The incident only became public two years later in 2015, and Mueller filed a defamation lawsuit against Taylor, which led her to filing a countersuit alleging sexual assault.

According to RAINN, the largest anti-sexual violence organisation in the US, statistics at the time showed that two out of three sexual assaults in the country went unreported. When it happened, Taylor and her mother did not go to the police to report the incident, and Taylor's lawyer remarked on this decision, saying she wanted to keep the incident "discreet and quiet and confidential." The civil proceedings were Taylor's opportunity to find her voice and fight back against Mueller.

Taylor's testimony was strongly praised by fans, particularly in the face of efforts by Mueller's lawyers to undermine her credibility. At one point, she was accused of misidentifying Mueller, and responded with: "I'm not going to allow you or your client to say I am to blame." On another occasion, she was asked why the now infamous photo, which was used as a key piece of evidence for the plaintiff, did not show the front of her skirt ruffled. She replied, defiantly: "Because my ass is located on the back of my body."

The trial marked a significant moment in the fight against sexual violence, particularly as Taylor only asked for a symbolic $1 in damages from Mueller. ▶▶

Taylor poses at the 2019 AMAs with her impressive haul of awards that year. Throughout her career so far, Taylor has received more than 930 award nominations and has won more than 430 of them.

Images: Getty

Taylor has inspired many young people, especially girls, to learn the guitar.

She explained her decision, saying, "I acknowledge the privilege that I benefit from in life, in society and in my ability to shoulder the enormous cost of defending myself in a trial like this." She added: "My hope is to help those whose voices should also be heard."

Fighting for fellow artists

As the music industry has moved towards a culture of streaming, Taylor's success is something of an anomaly: while record sales decline, her music has contributed to a rise in vinyl sales. To date, Taylor has sold more than 150 million singles worldwide, and is the second highest-certified female digital singles artist in the US with 134 million total units certified by the Recording Industry Association of America. *New York Magazine* wrote that her music's ability to drive sales make her "the one bending the music industry to her will," and musicologists Mary Fogarty and Gina Arnold named her "the last great rock star."

Despite this, Taylor has had to fight ferociously against the streaming titans to secure remuneration for herself and other artists. In November 2014, she removed her entire music catalogue from streaming service Spotify, and just over six months later, in June 2015, she wrote an open letter criticising Apple Music for not offering comprehensive remuneration to artists.

Although she re-added her music to Spotify, Amazon Music and Google Play in 2017, she continued to fight for artists' rights. In 2018, as part of her record deal with Universal Music, she demanded that the label must pay all artists a portion of money from its sales of Spotify shares in the future. *The Standard* called Swift "one of few artists with the power and profile to create change in the music world."

Taylor is also a huge supporter of the arts, and donated $75,000 to Nashville's Hendersonville High School in 2010 to help refurbish the school auditorium. Two years later, she pledged $4 million to fund a new education centre at the Country Music Hall of Fame and Museum in Nashville, and also donated $60,000, alongside textbook rental company Chegg, to the music departments of six universities in the US. Taylor gave $100,000 to the Nashville Symphony in 2013, and has made frequent donations ▶▶

Taylor's music videos, tour shows and other live performances are renowned for their spectacle and storytelling.

In May 2021, Taylor became the first female artist to be given the BRITs' highest accolade: the Global Icon Award.

Taylor and *All Too Well: The Short Film* star Sadie Sink at the Toronto International Film Festival in September 2022.

towards the advancement of children's literacy, pledging $250,000 in 2009 to various schools across the country, as well as 6,000 librarian-chosen books to the Reading Public Library in Pennsylvania, 14,000 to the Nashville Public Library in Tennessee, and 25,000 to schools in New York City.

Taking control

Similarly to her fight to secure more respect for artists, Taylor has regained control over her music catalogue and career in recent years, in several different ways. In 2020, she released her surprise album *folklore*, which she referred to as "a collection of songs and stories that flowed like a stream of consciousness." The album, and its sister record, *evermore*, marked an important shift for Taylor, by taking ownership of the album rollout and promotion process through surprise releases.

She has also been known to direct her own music videos, with the earliest being the visuals for 'I'm Only Me When I'm with You' in 2008, which showcased shots of her live concert footage. Other earlier examples include music videos for 'The Best Day' in 2009 – which incorporated home videos of Taylor and her mother– and 'Mine' in 2010. More recently, however, she directed the iconic videos for her LGBTQ+ anthem 'You Need to Calm Down', which featured an ensemble cast of queer icons, and a beautiful short film to accompany an extended re-recording of her song 'All Too Well', featuring actors Sadie Sink and Dylan O'Brien.

In June 2019, news broke that Scooter Braun had purchased her former record label, and on 1 July, she wrote an open letter, accusing Braun of being behind the (very public) bullying she had faced. In April 2020, her former record label Big Machine released *Live from Clear Channel Stripped 2008*, a live album of her performances at a 2008 radio show, which was not authorised by Taylor. Braun sold her masters, videos and artworks to Shamrock Holdings for $300 million, which led to Taylor beginning her work on re-recording her back catalogue from November 2020 onwards.

Taylor released the first re-recording of her back catalogue, *Fearless (Taylor's Version)*, in April 2021. The album became the first ever re-recorded album to peak at the number one spot on the *Billboard* 200. She released her second re-recorded album, *Red (Taylor's Version)* in November 2021, with a ten-minute version of 'All Too Well' serving as the album's promotional single, which debuted at the number one spot on the US *Billboard* Hot 100. At 10 minutes and 13 seconds, the track also broke the record for being the longest number one hit of all time – the long-standing record previously held since 1972 by Don McLean's 8-minute-37-second 'American Pie'.

Taylor is truly a trailblazer, proving herself to be an inspiration to both artists and fans alike. Her contributions to songwriting, various musical genres, and the music industry as a whole place her as one of the most iconic artists of her generation. As Taylor continues to evolve her sound, and takes on different projects, fans eagerly anticipate what is sure to be an exciting future for her.

Taylor and some of her *folklore* collaborators at the Grammys in March 2021. L-R: Laura Sisk, Jack Antonoff, Taylor, Aaron Dessner and Jonathan Low.

Images: Getty

89

"Her lyrics resonate across all generations, her songs touch everyone and her impact around the world is extraordinary.

Carole King presenting Taylor with the Artist of the Decade Award at the 2019 AMAs

She fights for musicians'
rights. She advocates for the
LGBTQ community, vocally and
with substantial philanthropy.
She never, ever, misses
an opportunity to call out
horrendous gender inequality in
this industry.

Jameela Jamil presenting Taylor with the
Woman of the Decade Award at *Billboard*'s
2019 Women in Music Event

Images: Getty

In 2021, Taylor became the first ever female recipient of the BRITs Icon Award. It is the organisation's highest accolade, reserved for truly exceptional artists, with previous winners being David Bowie, Elton John and Robbie Williams.

Taylor pictured with her *folklore* and *evermore* collaborators Jack Antonoff (left) and Aaron Dessner (right) at the Grammys in March 2021. Her two 2020 'lockdown' albums were met with great critical acclaim.

CHAPTER 5

Taylor wrote and directed the 2021 short film *All Too Well* starring Dylan O'Brien and Sadie Sink (above). It is based on the ten-minute version of Taylor's song of the same name.

Taylor performing at the Nashville Songwriter Awards where she was awarded the honour of Songwriter-Artist of the Decade in September 2021.

Images: Getty

95

"My hope for the future, not just in the music industry, but in every young girl I meet... is that they all realize their worth and ask for it.

Taylor Swift writing in the *Wall Street Journal*, 2014